We use machines (muh-SHEENS) every day. Machines help make our lives easier.

Some machines, such as lawn mowers and vacuum (VAK-yoom) cleaners, have many parts.

Lawn mower

Vacuum cleaner

These everyday things are simple machines.

Other machines have
few parts. They are
called simple machines.

Levers, inclined planes,
wheels and axles (AK-suls),
and pulleys are four kinds
of simple machines.

This bottle opener is a kind of lever. It helps you remove the cap from a bottle.

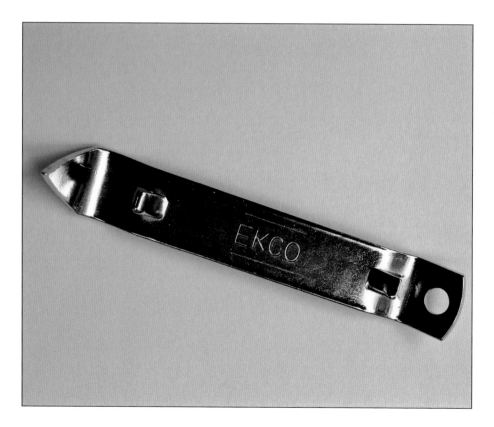

Some levers can help you move a heavy object, such as a rock.

Push down on one end of a lever. The other end moves up and pushes against whatever you are trying to move.

This boy is using a lever called a crowbar.

12

Have you ever ridden
a seesaw?

A seesaw is a kind of
lever. One side goes
up, while the other
side goes down.

Inclined planes are all around you.

A plane is just a flat surface, like a wooden board. An inclined plane is a flat surface that is slanted.

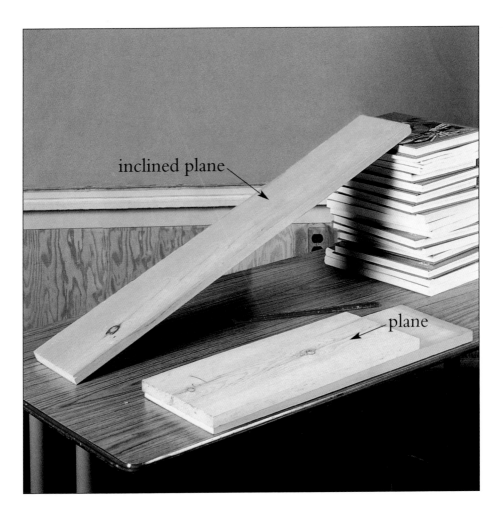

inclined plane

plane

15

Ramps are inclined planes.
It is easier to push a big load
up a ramp than to lift it.

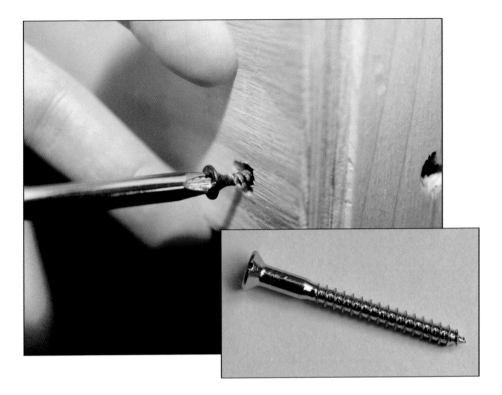

A screw is an inclined
plane wrapped around
a rod. Screws help hold
things together.

wedge

18

A wedge (wej) is another kind of inclined plane.

A wedge can help you cut wood. When a wedge is hit with a big hammer, its thin part splits the wood.

Wheels help things go.
An axle, or rod, connects
a pair of wheels. The axle
helps the wheels turn.

axle

Wheels are on bicycles
and cars.

It would be very hard
to move a bike or car
without wheels.

A pulley helps you lift heavy objects. A pulley's rope passes over a small wheel. Pull down on one end of the rope. You can lift a very heavy load tied to the other end.

pulley

pulley

A pulley can help you
raise and lower the flag
on a flagpole.

You can even lift the sail on a boat using a pulley.

These children are using two kinds of simple machines.

A wheelbarrow is a kind of lever, and it has wheels.

Have you used any simple machines today?

Words You Know

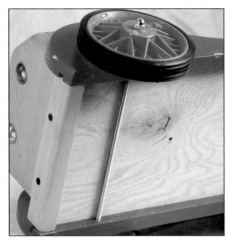

axle

inclined plane

lever

pulley

30

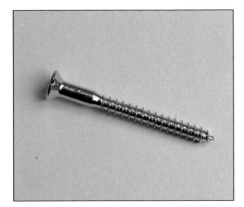

screw

seesaw

wedge

wheel

31

Index

About the Author

Allan Fowler is a freelance writer with a background in advertising.
Born in New York, he now lives in Chicago and enjoys traveling.

Photo Credits

Photographs ©: Dan Brody: 3, 5, 17, 23; Nance S. Trueworthy: cover, 6,
8, 17 inset, 31 top left; PhotoEdit: 22, 31 bottom right (Myrleen Ferguson),
11, 30 bottom left (Tony Freeman), 12, 24, 31 top right (Michael Newman),
4 (David Young-Wolff); Stock Boston: 16, 26, 29 (Bob Daemmrich), 9, 15,
30 top right (Stephen Frisch), 25, 30 bottom right (Paul Mozell); Superstock,
Inc.: 18, 31 bottom left; Tony Stone Images: 27 (Laurence Monneret);
Unicorn Stock Photos: 21, 30 top left (Wayne Floyd).